MORE PRAISE FOR SALES TEAM LEADERSHIP: PURE AND SIMPLE

This book is the result of years of personal sales, team, and leadership experiences.

"I have read dozens of sales books and have attended just as many seminars. It was hard to imagine what else there was left to say … until I read Coach Joe Sasso's book. The wisdom here is pure, inspiring, and game-changing. It is delivered in a very edible way with stories, data, and 'what now' next steps. This will change you and how you plan on making magic happen with your customers."

Dr. Izzy Justice
CEO of EQ Mentor and author of *EPowerment*

"The marketplace is dynamic and ever changing. Pure and Simple provides a play-by-play formula for leaders to drive results. Coach Joe's focus on accountability is sorely needed in today's business world. No one does it alone; it takes leaders in all phases of the team's performance. The coaching tips in this book are achievable by those who want to win!"

Jack Plating
Retired Executive Vice President and
Chief Operating Officer, Verizon Wireless

"I have lived the Sales Team Leadership business experience. Early in my sales career, it was about me—making sales, reaching and exceeding quota, becoming better in my profession. I did these things and enjoyed the financial rewards and achievement accolades. However, my company adopted a team approach for sales with our customers. As in this book, team members sharing knowledge and comparing information on our competitors, the marketplace, and process improvements provided a pathway to industry leadership. Our 'value-added' components were always something none of our competitors could match. Experiences of the 'team' concept led me from 'me' to 'we,' which provided a most rewarding career experience."

Wayne Teas
Mortgage Banker, Guaranty Bank

"Pure and Simple *will help many teams inside and outside of sales become more productive and successful. I really enjoyed the concepts that Coach Joe communicated through his writing, storytelling, and visuals. So many great books leave you asking yourself, 'Where do I start and how?' Not this book. Coach Joe gives readers well-defined steps that are easy to apply so your team can 'Spiral Up' to new heights.*"

Thea Noel
Employment Coordinator, Goodwill of Georgia

"Sales Team Leadership: Pure and Simple *should be required reading for all people working on teams. Accessibility with open communications is often a critical discipline leaders fail to practice. It is always a great concern because many leaders get caught up in all the daily routines and operational demands of the business. As a result, they tend to minimize the importance and criticality of making time to be proactively accessible with customers, employees, and their peers. I am encouraged by the continual engagement of the team in this book. I can't recommend it enough. Coach Joe's book is definitely for new salespeople, and it should be read by all established 'pros' who know that 'back to basics' is a strategic key for every success.*"

Gustavo Arenas
Retired Senior VP and Chief Sales Officer, AMD

"*There is an old saying something to the effect of 'we don't know what we know.'* Pure and Simple *presents the way for clarifying what we all know are successful principles for sales and teamwork success. If you are just getting into the selling game, or managing a team, or leading a team of people, or even if you're an already established professional, you will find great value in what Coach Joe has to say. Follow up and do the practices he points to from experience and you will reach your success. Continuous improvement is a lifelong journey, and this book fits perfectly.*"

Randal Davis
Vice President Coffee Service Div, Red Diamond, Inc.

"*From creating a vision, to effective execution and peak team performance, all the steps clearly lead to outstanding team achievement. The nuggets from real experiences in Coach Joe's Journal are invaluable. This book is a must read for both the very successful sales team leader and those just starting their journey in sales and teamwork. Kyle's successful journey flows. Let the spiral be your guide. You and your team will achieve leadership success.*"

Tom Reichart
Vice President Business Development, Mercury Payment Systems

"*The framework that Coach Joe presents is clear and concise. The principles outlined are essential if you are to achieve sales team leadership. Coach Joe's insights and storytelling make this a book that can be read and understood quickly by everyone who wants to do well as a sales team leader.*"

Jeffrey L. Krug
President, J. L. Krug & Associates, Inc.

SALES TEAM LEADERSHIP:
PURE AND SIMPLE

BY COACH JOE SASSO

iUniverse, Inc.
Bloomington

iUniverse books may be ordered through booksellers or by contacting:

iUniverse
1663 Liberty Drive
Bloomington, IN 47403
www.iuniverse.com
1-800-Authors (1-800-288-4677)

ISBN: 978-1-4697-8964-4 (sc)
ISBN: 978-1-4697-8966-8 (hc)
ISBN: 978-1-4697-8965-1 (e)

Printed in the United States of America

iUniverse rev. date: 3/22/2012

DEDICATION

To my wife, Carol,
our family's mutually trusting coach, mentor,
and "fan in the stands"
and to the memory of
Warren Clary and Bill Bang,
your spirits are still alive in me
and they are in this book.

Twenty-five percent of the profits from the sale of this book will be donated to St. Jude's Children's Research Hospital in Memphis, Tennessee.

TABLE OF CONTENTS

Acknowledgments...xiii
Foreword xv

FORMING—COMPLIMENTARY
TALENTS FOR A COMMON CAUSE

Chapter 1   "Success Breeds Success" Is Not a Given!..............3
Chapter 2   Fear Is Knowing That I Don't Know!.....................9

STORMING—DISRUPTIVE CHALLENGES
TO THE COMMON UNITY

Chapter 3   Becoming Better Is a Choice...................................21
Chapter 4   Preview Commitment: Necessary for *All* Successful
             Reviews 27
Chapter 5   Team Collaboration Unifies and Strengthens Every
             Member...33
Chapter 6   Mutual Growth Generates Unlimited Opportunities.....37
Chapter 7   Ownership Is Accountability *Now!*......................43

PERFORMING—EXTRORDINARY
TIMES DURING TEAM UNITY

Chapter 8   Emerging Team Member Leadership 53
Chapter 9   Effectiveness: Achieving Mutual Growth.................57
Chapter 10   Speeding Synchronously...63

METAMORPHOSIS—TRANSCENDING THE EMBRYO OF "ME"

Chapter 11 Benefits of the New "WE" 71
Chapter 12 Afterword 77

MEGA-METAMORPHOSIS—"WE" EQUALS MANY AND NEW BREAKTHROUGHS

Chapter 13 We Are All Leaders 83
Bonus Material... 85

ACKNOWLEDGMENTS

This is the culmination of years of relationships with many great people who I have worked alongside of as peers, managers, leaders, and team members. Most notably in recent months I have received valuable insights about the book from Dr. W. Carl Joiner, Professor Emeritus, Mercer University and Don Holt, retired VP, Sales Manager and Sales Leader, Motorola Inc. Many thanks also to the editors and people who have assisted me in the editing and for the quality polishing of this book from iUniverse publishing company.

FOREWORD

If you are a new salesperson or a new sales manager, this book is for you. If you're a seasoned sales pro or seasoned professional sales manager and leader, this book will raise your awareness of what your experiences have taught you. At the same time it will challenge you to be better than ever before.

As the old adage says, "Amateurs compete with amateurs. Pros compete with themselves." We all know that on the best-performing sales teams, all members—including the proven pros—consciously challenge each other to be winning members on the "one winning team."

This book focuses on teams Coach Joe has served on as a salesman, sales manager, and sales team leader. "Being adept at adapting" during these fast, furious, and challenging economic times means sales teamwork must be intentionally focused on becoming better and better based on the growing knowledge and experiences of the whole team. Teamwork today demands diversity and, at the same time, inclusion of all members. Focus on the vision as mission; communications moment to moment; faster exchanges between team members; strategies executed more easily for the greatest impact while controlling costs; team members who understand the risks needed to be taken for the anticipated rewards to be gained by their cumulative actions; team members who challenge and help complete each other to be better and better; and, finally and most importantly, team members who have mutual trust and work for the mutual benefit of the whole team winning.

Pure and Simple, then, is about Making Sales Happen Right the First Time—Right Now!

Ed DeCosta, Chief Catalyst, Catalyst Associates, LLC
Faculty, John Maxwell Leadership Certification Team

FORMING—
COMPLIMENTARY
TALENTS FOR A
COMMON CAUSE

CHAPTER ONE

"Success Breeds Success" Is Not a Given!

The person who gets the farthest is generally the one who is willing to do and dare. The sure-thing boat never gets far from shore.

Dale Carnegie

Every professional focuses on the continuous goal of being better and more successful in business. At the outset, what the ultimate success will be is never completely known. Circumstances present new opportunities and challenges that propel people upward to their ultimate success.

THE PROMOTION

Kyle proved himself as a successful salesman and was promoted to sales manager. He quickly understood his role as manager and became an effective working coach with his sales team. With smart, continuous efforts and accountability for his actions, he became a well-known and respected executive in several business networks. From time to time, interested companies courted him, but he remained happy and continued to be successful right where he was. One day he received an offer he couldn't ignore; and after much deliberation with his company leaders, Kyle accepted the new company's offer. He departed under the best of circumstances, knowing he would be missed.

DANGER IN OPPORTUNITY: SPIRALING DISCOVERIES OF THE RISKS FOR THE REWARD

Kyle's new assignment was to lead an already successful sales team that was facing a growing number of competitors who were challenging their continuing success. The previous sales manager had ridden on the successes of the sales team and left without notice for another company. Kyle knew that one of the greatest challenges for a sales manager can be the success of a previous manager because the new manager is always expected to continue the upward spiral to more and greater business successes. It is better to take on the challenge of a business when the business is down because, in truth, there is nowhere to go but up. Kyle knew this and accepted the challenge anyway.

Kyle had worked his way up through the ranks before knowing that a professional always competes with himself first. He was a consummate student of lifelong learning. Most important, serving others or the team was without a doubt his best character trait. Kyle knew that being a part of something greater than himself always led to improvements in himself and improvements in others. However, serving and giving so much also has its pitfalls. You can be easily taken advantage of and lose in an extremely competitive environment if things don't work out. Yet, Kyle also knew the rewards would have more energizing effects. The possibility of building and developing himself with other successful businesspeople far outweighed the fear of any loss. At this point in Kyle's professional career, the new job had its risks, but they were far outweighed when he considered the rewards. Ultimately, the opportunities and challenges of the new job were about growth and moving upward with a new team.

Previously Kyle had sold business to business, that is, directly to customers who used the products he sold. In his new assignment he would be selling through distributors who sold to their customers.

At the first meeting, Kyle was introduced to the sales team with the usual pomp and circumstance that you would expect for a proven and successful sales manager. As a result, Kyle was sought out personally throughout the day and welcomed with personal best wishes by every team member. It was unbelievable, he thought, that everyone was on target to reach his or her own individual sales goals. Everyone was happy, but he sensed that everyone had a guarded indifference about the team performance, because everyone only cared about his or her own efforts. There was a minimum of concern about their competition or the way the sales were being won.

Maintaining sales performance wasn't the easy answer. This was not just misplaced good fortune; he was not simply being asked to do more of the same. There was an arrogance, an attitude of "We're number one," about their company victories over external competition—while at the same time, there was greater concern about the internal competition: "*I'm* number one!" Their concern was misplaced arrogance on themselves as opposed to the team. Kyle knew it. But did they know and understand it? Kyle knew this was not a sales team! But could it *become* a sales team? Kyle knew he needed to understand a lot more about what the salespeople were currently doing and not doing. He needed to know how his leadership could make a difference; otherwise, he wasn't needed—and for that matter, maybe the sales team wasn't needed either. Could they all be replaced by a direct order entry system with the distributors?

COACH JOE'S JOURNAL

It is very important for anyone who wants to get ahead in business to grow and maintain his or her network of business associates. Being active in national industry networks will also help generate and cultivate business insights on trends and changes that can positively or negatively impact your business. It is very important to keep growing and maintaining your local networks. It affords you the opportunity to receive and exchange leads and referrals for the continued growth of your business.

As success breeds success, it is also true that a downturn in business can result in apathy and malaise of good business practices. A manager just pushing people harder to perform is not the answer. Another mistake made on poorly performing teams is the thinking that you simply need more people. But if you try to add people to a team that doesn't understand why it is not having success, the members usually become self-centered and don't want anyone taking over what they feel are the results of their efforts in their territories, no matter how good or bad their results. Breaking

---

this cultural habit is difficult because of the team's self-centered focus on keeping their success going—and lack of focus on others. Individual competitive drive stifles, or even stops, continued progress because people think that cutting into their own areas of responsibility means giving up something, which may affect their income.

This bottom-line mentality is not only at the micro level of the individual; it can be at the macro level of the company as well. Success that only works for the individual never breaks through to higher levels of performance because it is carnivorous to the point of eating its own. Remember, amateurs compete with amateurs, while pros compete with themselves. Similarly, professional teams develop and learn to compete with themselves at higher levels, pressing for better and better performances.

UNLEARNING "ME" AND LEARNING "WE"

One key to a successful team mentality is moving from "me" to "we." Having team members who genuinely care about one another's overall success is an important element in building a team that works together. Here is a summary of those points:

Diminishing "Me"	Thriving "We"
WIIFM: What's in it for me?	WIIFW: What's in it for we (the team)?
Silence: No questions asked	Communications: Open, clarifying, collaborative
Purpose: I only do what I need to do	Purpose: Vision and unity
Goals: I make mine	Goals: Our team in collaboration
Personal Direction: Just doing my thing	Team Leadership Within: How can I contribute?
Just pay me for the work I do	Involvement: Effective and accountable
Survival: It's just about me!	Mutual Trust: Mutually beneficial contributions

Figure 1. Me versus We Elements

Survival lessons have been deeply ingrained in the learning styles of many businesses today. Businesses continue to try and overcome the crippling self-centered "silo" mentality of command and control without whole team accountability; it's not just about *me* anymore. Businesses that are succeeding by diminishing *me* and emphasizing *we* are beginning to unlearn the "survival of the fittest" mentality. The internal business is not about competition; it is about collaboration. Mutual collaboration within a team or organization involves cooperating at the highest level for continuous improvement and growth. Everyone works together, finding much better ways to prosper because of their vision and openness, as well as their unifying and mutually collaborating spirit. Their expectations of great outcomes of reward are equal to their great understanding of the risks of doing business today.

CHAPTER TWO

Fear Is Knowing That I Don't Know!

Without a plan, any effort results in a reward or a failure, but either way, we can't take the credit. As Thoreau said, "The mass of men lead lives of quiet desperation. What is called desperation is confirmed resignation." Planning is hard work! Once again, the old adage is correct: "Plan your work, and work your plan." The resulting strategies and tactics have their ups and downs, but they always lead to continuous improvements along the way.

If Kyle was to survive and succeed as the new manager of the sales team, he needed to know more about what the team was doing and, more important, what they were not doing. He needed to know more about how to plan for greater success and impact with the customers. Then he needed to plan how to develop and improve the performance of the sales team to achieve more.

SWOT ANALYSIS

Kyle started with a SWOT analysis. A SWOT analysis is a strategic planning method used to evaluate the **s**trengths, **w**eaknesses, **o**pportunities, and **t**hreats involved in a business. It involves specifying the objective of the business and identifying the internal and external factors that are favorable and unfavorable to achieving that objective. The technique is credited to Albert Humphrey, who led a convention at Stanford University in the 1960s and 1970s using data from Fortune 500 companies.

- **S**trengths: characteristics of the business or team that give it an advantage over others in the industry
- **W**eaknesses: characteristics that place the team at a disadvantage relative to others
- **O**pportunities: *external* chances to have greater success, or make greater sales or profits in the environment
- **T**hreats: *external* elements in the environment that could cause trouble for the business

SWOT analysis is essential to subsequent steps in the process of planning and development for achievement. The SWOT analysis is a good place to start and a continuous vital element in any business's successful planning. The number-one goal for a sales team is to sell the products and services expected by the company. The overall goal becomes known by the sales team simply as "quota." *Quota* is the minimum expected sales volume by which the team can successfully maintain itself. The team's assigned sales quota is broken down, and portions are distributed to each salesperson.

STRENGTHS

To start his SWOT analysis, Kyle began with team member interviews. He interviewed the sales leaders first. Everyone was knowledgeable and could provide valuable information about what was working well, as well as his or her perceptions about what could make the team better. Kyle's job as sales manager was to compile the information so he could better understand how to plan and develop strategies. He quickly confirmed and understood that the products

- were in high demand by the distributors;
- had the best marketing;
- were branded as the best;
- were designed for easy installation;
- were supported by a responsive customer service team;
- had a sales force that outnumbered the competition ten to one; and
- provided an immediate return on investment, essentially selling themselves.

Kyle now knew why the team felt invincible. These product strengths were superior to all other offerings. But that superiority doesn't justify a smug "We're number one" attitude. That attitude breeds complacency, as it can become the Achilles' heel that can lead to any team's or company's death spiral.

WEAKNESSES

The distributors' nightmare was keeping the shelves stocked with product. The growth and demand for the product was so great that the company's manufacturing team could not manufacture and ship the product fast enough. This problem caused the distributors to demand scheduling confirmation, which increased supervision and continuous confirmation of product shipments. To compensate for this, the salespeople had become babysitters to the manufacturing scheduling system. The sales team bore the burden of the distributors' distress over the lack of available product and was the recipient of their threats when schedules were blown or changed without notice because of material shortages. The salespeople kept pressure on the manufacturing team to build more products faster by over forecasting higher sales volume. If there was good news at all, it was that sales records were being broken all the time; however, not meeting delivery commitments was the bad news. The lack of integrity was generating silos of mistrust that were undermining relationships within both the company's manufacturing and sales operations.

Lack of confidence in the shipping schedule led to a downward spiral of distributor trust with the whole company. This was confirmed by the distributors whom Kyle interviewed, who noted these as the two biggest weaknesses the company and sales team faced. Ultimately the inability to deliver products on time and on schedule was born out by the sales team, who were in constant communication with the distributors. This, in turn, led to threats to end their relationships. Every minute spent babysitting was an erosion of their professional ability to protect the return on investment for their distributors. This resulted in the sales team making future promises that the issues wouldn't happen again. If mistrust in relationships like this kept happening, this weakness could lead to a death spiral. Competitors given the chance to develop a better trusting relationship with the distributors could make Kyle's team the big losers!

In manufacturing's defense, it must be noted that there were times when the business would slow down and they had to hold inventory while the distributors were slow or the forecasts had been overinflated. But this was rare for the most part, as business was very strong. No matter how Kyle reviewed the situation, it was a terrible waste of the salespeople's time. Professional salespeople were being abused. This loss of distributor confidence in the salesperson led to remarks by the distributors that they felt disadvantaged and abused.

These weaknesses were more than alarming; left unchecked, they could destroy the company when the right competitor got its act together. Distributors would flock to the competition for spite because they had been disadvantaged for so long in the past. This last point was actually a threat to the company's future. The weakness, then, was the whole company's unbridled current success. If this weakness wasn't changed, the downward spiral could bring the company to its knees—if not its death.

OPPORTUNITIES

Born out of ideas, challenges, problems, and threats, Kyle saw opportunities to improve.

In one of Kyle's first meetings with a leading distributor, the number-one complaint was not as much delivery as it was price. Business was so good that, when the distributor was out of stock, they bought from other competitors. Not so surprisingly, the price was lower, and the product worked. In spite of the competitors' lacking marketing and brand acceptance, the customers bought the alternative product because it worked.

Selling the competitors' products was tougher for the distributors, but they were meeting with success. The competitors offset these problems with increases in co-op advertising and rebate money. To overcome these threats, Kyle's company could offer more local advertising, co-op efforts, and rebates to slow down the competition. But there were no guarantees. Kyle knew the sales team would only be matching the competition. Leadership was needed if the sales team was to be successful in maintaining and growing the company's share of the market.

Kyle understood that the salesperson's number-one success was in his or her value-added personal service to the distributor. The salespeople outnumbered their competition. They provided the distributors with a direct link and a level of trust with the company. They would do almost anything the distributors asked them to do. These contributing factors were allowing them to maintain higher prices for their products as long as delivery kept improving and they could keep the distributors' shelves stocked with their products. Everyone knew, even though their product was preferred, that price was the slippery slope. It would definitely be eroding faster as more competitors entered the market and built up their business resources, so this opportunity also had a threat.

THREATS

The biggest challenge facing the sales team was finding ways to continue growing the distributor business while maintaining and growing company market share. Any complacency by the team to just meet or beat competitive prices would result in a death spiral. Kyle was only interested in a spiral that would grow and expand upward. There seemed to be no limits as long as Kyle's sales team met the distributors' purchasing demands. Success meant they could maintain their premium price as long as value grew and quality was maintained. *Critical to all this success was a need for a resurgence of value-added, continuous improvement in the relationships the salespeople had with the distributors. The challenge was finding ways to improve those relationships by doing the right things, doing those things right the first time, and doing those right things now.*

After investigation and reflection, Kyle became aware that the biggest threat was not that his job was vulnerable, but that the whole sales team could be eliminated and replaced with an automated entry system in the hands of the distributors. This could be done if the competition found ways to chip away at pricing, delivery schedules, and other improvements in their operations. Kyle's own company would be relieved of overhead as they removed salespeople from the operation. This threat was real, but it was not an Achilles' heel. As long as relationships reinforced good business practices, the team would be building on a foundation of business successes. In Kyle's mind, it followed that the sales team had to be a sales team that knew how to do business more successfully.

Once his SWOT analysis was completed, Kyle quickly discovered that the previous sales manager's vision was simply this: "We sell more because we are the biggest and we're the best! Be available when your distributor calls, write orders, keep their shelves stocked, and keep bugging the factory 'til they ship what your customer needs!"

No wonder there was an excess of pride! The sales team thought they made the business happen because of their dedication and hard work with the distributors. They were invincible. They couldn't lose—and if they did lose, it wasn't their fault! While the vision had some validity because the company was big and had the best reputation and the biggest sales team, it was just too individually ego-inflating to assume that each salesperson was the best and that any failure would never be his or her fault! Ultimately this type of salesperson grows lazy in his or her order-taker status.

Kyle knew this current shallow perception of how the business was evolving, along with a lack of vision, was a bottomless sinkhole for the sales team. He was finding new lifelines for development.

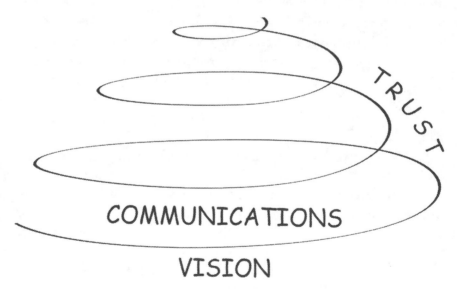

Figure 2. Vision, Communication, and Trust

Vision spirals up with communications that are consistently trustful, with the exchange of good, bad, and difficult information. It's about doing it right, with trust, the first time. As the team moves up the spiral, encompassing trust is the accelerator for faster sales rep and sales team breakthrough success.

VISION: YOUR GRASP MUST BE
BEYOND YOUR REACH

Kyle needed a vision that would generate new life in the team if his leadership was to be effective. He had to plant a vision in the minds of the sales team about what success would mean in the future. Their performance to date had been on par with other sales teams in the country. The team was satisfied to be average, in the middle of the pack. Standing out as number one and the leader in the country was not a team vision. The company had its basic business vision for success: increase revenue; build new customers while maintaining existing customers; and keep costs down. Great vision starts on the foundation that is a seemingly impossible intention; that is imaginative, new, and bold; and that unites team members in knowing it can be accomplished. A great, inspiring vision creates the passion within. It ignites the fire that energizes everyone. And finally, vision generates momentum by refusing to be extinguished until the vision is achieved.

Kyle understood enough now to know that the sales team needed his leadership to continue to build and maintain the best business relationships within their own company and with the distributors they served. At the same time, they needed to find new value-added competitive business edges that would enable them to keep generating mutually profitable sales for themselves and for their distributors. Distributor relationships were important to ensure that the sales team had a solid foundation with reinforcement for continuous growth.

Kyle knew the vision was not to just become the number-one sales team in the company, but to be a new and bold representation that would stand out in the imagination of the company and their distributors. It would be a stretch, but the sales team had to become the number-one business sales team. Reaching for and grasping number one in sales would require each and every one's best business sense and sales performance. All business successes would have to be mutual successes: of the team, the company, and the business distributors.

Kyle began openly communicating, pushing and nurturing the vision that the team includes all members as business partners. The sales team had to want it with all their senses. The more they sought potential opportunities for business success, the more they operated with passion about the business being mutually rewarding for their distributors and their company. The key to their spiraling success was being more total-business oriented. The more they focused on the total business, the more they would become a "business sales team."

COACH JOE'S JOURNAL

While selling electronic equipment, such as cell phones, pagers, and an assortment of accessories through distributors, it was my experience that competitive products sold more often when our distributors were out of our stock. This caused an erosion of market share and bolstered the competition because they were able to move their products. Our competitive strategy was to always to keep the distributors' shelves stocked with an abundance of our products.

An important distinction for sales success is to build in value-added customer product features as well as service advantages for the customer, such as a toll-free help-desk line or a service feature for the distributor that allows them to return defective product without priorities, delays, or any hassle. Value-added products and services are success strategies and activities that show the quality and care delivered by the manufacturing operations. They are a means by which a company exhibits a very strong relationship, first through the salespeople and then through the backing of the whole company. Ultimately this generates an influence within the distributor's company, as the distributor's employees in turn prefer and recommend the company's products over those of the competition.

Our relationship was successfully modeled as a business partnership. We built quasi partnering arrangements by being a working member of distributors' business teams. It was hard and smart work. Our business relationship was far ahead of the competition. We were number one in investigating and implementing value-added product features and services. This strategy helped us successfully maintain and grow our business with the distributors we served.

The weakness in Kyle's company relates to a time when business is booming. This may seem farfetched compared to the economy we are in today; however, it remains true that if you can't keep the distributors' shelves stocked with your products, you run the risk of reducing sales and ceding market share to the competition. To avoid the risk of losses in today's economy, it is most important that open and shared communications reflect the utmost level of trust. No one likes bad news, but the integrity of communications is imperative for success in business.

The most successful team I had the privilege to work with generated a renewable and sustaining personal and team vision every quarter. We listened to our customers and to what our company's leaders were seeking to accomplish. It wasn't always easy to find this out. We had to constantly be investigating what we could do more of, change, hand off, or eliminate. In some cases, as we gave more of ourselves, it began to look like we were going to put ourselves out of business. However, that never happened. In the end it created a loyalty with our distributor leaders and their teams that we learned to appreciate and expect. We were valued by all as we kept striving to be better and better at what we were doing. Our efforts for a conscious vision and then working it kept us in good favor—spiraling up—with our customers and the leaders of our company.

It is easier to take a team from the bottom and move it up than to improve a successful team. When the team is already achieving successes, the salespeople may enjoy too much perceived success to realize that they aren't at their peak performance. Moving a good team beyond this plateau is the work of a new leader starting with a challenging, new, and improved vision. The new vision challenges the team to reinvent itself in a way that motivates and results in new actions. A great team loves what they are doing together. They develop a spirit for the work they love to do together. They become oblivious to time. Time flies as they operate on the cusp of innovation and creativity. The change and the spirit of the new invigorate them to keep spiraling up to ever-ascending heights of team successes.

STORMING—
DISRUPTIVE CHALLENGES TO THE COMMON UNITY

CHAPTER THREE

Becoming Better Is a Choice

Once Kyle had his vision for the sales team being a business sales team, he began to hold regular team meetings. Before Kyle's hire, salespeople had been required to send in two sales reports: an activity report that reported on the previous week's sales and a sales plan that showed their intended sales calls and results for the new week. Previously, these two reports were expected on the manager's desk by 8:00 a.m. Monday morning. Because they were so successful, the sales team had lost this discipline. Excuses for reports not being on time were more the norm, and reports were sketchy and haphazardly put together. Kyle knew he needed these timely reports to review successes of the past and organize for successful actions in the future. This change had to occur immediately to manage and coach the sales team.

Kyle began having everyone attend Monday morning sales meetings. The storm was brewing. The salespeople complained about not being able to start the week working with their customers. The truth was that everyone was comfortable operating independently. They enjoyed the autonomy they had with their distributors. Kyle felt these excuses were just a smoke screen. These self-serving attitudes were shallow; they were stifling business growth. There was no motivation to start the week with strong commitments for sales. Waiting for customers to call or just dropping by the distributor was not a plan, let alone an organized effort to grow a business that needed sales every week.

Kyle started the Monday morning meetings by pointing to the team vision—to become the number-one business sales team—and asking everyone if they had the intention, desire, and belief required to become members of the number-one business sales team in the country. He wanted to make sure that everyone understood and shared the challenges of what the vision meant. To accomplish this, he started by sharing results of his SWOT analysis with the sales team:

- Strengths: Best product, biggest sales team, best service and support, great ROI
- Weaknesses: erosion of distributor trust and confidence, price erosion, competitors growing and getting better, constant inventory shortages, delivery schedule discrepancies
- Opportunities: salespeople becoming business sales consultants to their distributors, point of sale and local advertising, co-op, rebates, best scheduling results
- Threats: growth of competition (obvious), loss of market share, price erosion, less profitable sales, and (most alarming) the elimination of company salespeople

The last point was a lightning rod with a thunder clap that got everyone's attention. Initially, there was fright and reluctance when Kyle asked for further suggestions and comments. Kyle knew he had to lead the way. The attitude of the team was one of personal concern. "Job loss! No way. Not mine!" Rather than a positive attitude of commitment by the salesperson to do whatever was needed to improve the situation. Kyle started by quoting Samuel Smiles: "Character is power more than knowledge is power." Power first generates from a strong character—when you knowingly commit to apply learned knowledge.

"Strength of character coupled with intention and commitment to apply more business knowledge to our sales business will have the effect of growing our sales team into a business sales team," Kyle said. "We will start and renew ourselves to become powerful and valuable partners of character with our distributors. We will commit to be more business knowledgeable, timely, and involved with our business and with our distributors' business so we can generate business growth for our continuing and future mutual prosperity."

Still alarmed and somewhat apprehensive, the salespeople began to open up. The discussions got stormy at points, but ultimately everyone began to get the message. The threat to their business and their sales positions was real. A software order entry system in the hands of the distributor could eliminate them all. People began to understand why Kyle had been purposefully laying out reasons even before this meeting as to why they needed to have a new vision of who they were and what they were doing for their distributors, for the company, and for themselves.

After a long discussion, there was agreement and reinforcement on all the issues. The company was beating the competition in their area. However, they knew the competition had opportunities to capture sales because the market was growing. A commitment to becoming the number-one business sales team was required. **Every team member had a new commitment:** *to add value by becoming business sales consultant partners who were committed to being in a continuously improving business relationship with distributors.*

Kyle went on to explain that salespeople without an understanding of their customer's business tend to push, pull, and sell their products without ever knowing if all the benefits they perceive are the only benefits every customer wants and needs. A business sales consultant on the other hand starts out as an investigator, attempting to understand how the customer does business. Questioning for understanding is the first step in knowing how products can help potential customers realize benefits that improve their bottom line. A business consultant is closer to being a partner than an outside salesperson just scheduling and delivering product. The best sales consultants can predict what the return on investment will be for the company that uses its products.

Kyle reinforced the business consultant idea by saying, "We started with our own strengths, weaknesses, opportunities, and threats; now, as consultants, we need to do the same with each of our distributors. The more we engender strong character and gain knowledge, the more power we will have to add value to their businesses. As business consultants we will become vital assets—*partners* to our distributors' businesses. Strategies and actions can then be formulated to keep both them and us on a spiraling growth curve, going up and up, for future successes."

As Kyle finished and the sales team got more excited about being consultants, the topic switched to how to win more customers for the distributors. It was a good conclusion to the meeting, and Kyle took note of a few who still were not ready for this change. He knew he had work to do to manage the change, but the majority of the team was on board and that was what Kyle wanted.

Attitude Defines Environment, Environment Defines Outcomes
John Maxwell

Kyle was feeling good about the meeting. With the process understood and agreed on by almost everyone, Kyle's intentions now changed for further improvements.

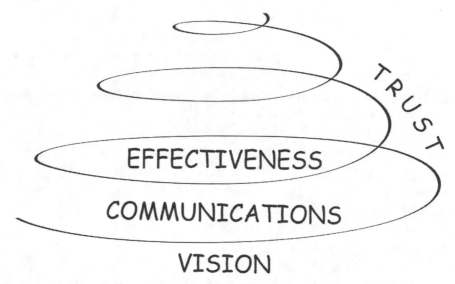

**Figure 3. Vision and Communications Leading
to Effectiveness Surrounded by Trust**

The catalyst for effectiveness evolves from doing the right thing to doing it now.

CHAPTER FOUR

Preview Commitment:
Necessary for *All* Successful Reviews

When you meet the unprepared with preparation, you are victorious.

Robert Pino

After the initial meeting, Kyle felt it was important for the team to grow in their trust—not only their trust in Kyle, but their trust in each other as well. Salespeople are always competitive and are usually guarded about what they share. Remember, *"Amateurs compete with amateurs, but the pros compete with themselves."* Everyone took individual pride in being number one. But now this individual view had to be expanded to a team perspective: *"We're* number one." The business information exchange was going to be vital to everyone's success and to the team's success. Kyle wanted the team members to be great outside competitors, while also learning and sharing their competitive edges internally with all the team members. To be successful, the trust objective had to unlock and open the competitive nature of everyone on the team for winning more sales: *become internally collaborative and externally competitive.* To accomplish this objective, each team member needed to understand the personal success benefits of sharing. Plain and simple: trust surrounds and spirals up when team members share strategies and actions with team members. It all adds to the winning bottom line for every team member.

People who exchange trust are innately and always willing to be held accountable for the actions they believe in and are committed to doing. The 'storming stage' causes them to dig deep within their personal beliefs. It becomes a period of acceptance based on their desire to know and confirm their beliefs or to change for the better based on the team's sometimes very stormy exchanges. This open, unabashed sharing, giving, and receiving among members elevates trust to its highest level. "We" now know each other's desire is to generate greater success for the collective, all of us. At this elevation, we instinctively know we are in the spirit of mutual trust.

When salespeople work in common unity toward mutual goals, their team meetings are the catalyst for learning and generating challenges, while discovering ways to overcome problems in a growing harmony that accelerates and compounds their business experiences. This experience in the safety of the team becomes a model for their work relationships with their distributors. Kyle knew the team needed to focus on both the internal and external environments, changing the mind-set from *me* to *we* and from *them* to *us*!

At the start of the Monday morning meetings, Kyle opened with a challenging team question: "What are we learning now that we should be doing more of to keep—and continue to grow—our business and our distributors' businesses now and in the future?" Initial responses were always a good starting point and demonstrated that the question was becoming an indelible, conscious question, challenging and raising the business competency level of every team member. Kyle wanted it that way because he knew it would be driving value-added business instincts everywhere and all the time.

Kyle's next step was to recognize the best sales performances of the past week. After that he would recognize and reinforce the growing strengths of the business with the best value-added awards for special contributions of the past week. This was definitely about extra effort that built the business and the relationships with customers. There was no limit on the number of awards and recognitions. More ideas generated more value-added efforts. This could be a new product seminar or a special sales incentive day with the distributor's team, meeting and working with their customers—any business activity that generated better business and better relationships. This part of the meeting was an emotional high for everyone. It elevated their levels of healthy, internal personal wins for the team. Once this important part of the meeting was completed, Kyle would then ask his team members to keep these winning moves on their mind as the Monday meeting progressed. He encouraged them to avoid interruptions and to take notes so they could be proactive as actively involved business team members.

Everyone was asked to present their individual reviews first. Everyone shared copies of their past week's activity and planning goals for the new week to the entire team.

The review of the past week's information was simple cause and effect. It was sales planned for and sales achieved or not achieved. This was a good time for 'war stories' that emphasized value-added success strategies and actions to win the business. The tales were usually about overcoming a business problem or meeting a business challenge with a win or just simply beating the competition. As information and explanations were presented, sales quota performance of each salesperson was made known.

Figure 4. Preview, Commitment, and Review Spiraling Up with Trust

The environment was challenging. After this brief review came the preview for the new week. Preview or planning is often just a "good intention." Salespeople are adept at goal setting, that is, presenting positive reports on what they intend to do. However, Kyle explained that in their new meeting format, this would be different when it came to an individual salesperson's plan for the new week. Prospective business was to be presented, and the planned intention for successes would be revealed to the entire sales team. If the performance goal was on target for achieving sales quota, the salesperson would explain the foundation for his or her belief. The team would then be allowed to question the team member for better understanding, as well as make suggestions to build on, reinforce, or change the preview. This preview would be a learning and growing business sales environment for the entire team. Everyone began to understand that the previews were complex, value added, and different from just the old way of setting goals. This is true leadership by every team member. Kyle knew that once they knew and understood this, they would begin to coach and support each other for results and for the total success of the business.

Effectiveness pushes the preview process to the forefront of sales achievement. Preview recognizes that the commitment is a well thought-out risk-and-reward plan by the team member. Review, pure and simple, confirms the success of the trust in the preview process. It bolsters and reinforces the team's confidence in the accountable performance of the team member. *Preview is coaching. It always ranks among the highest reasons why salespeople and sales teams are effective in achieving their sales goals. Preview, therefore, develops personal leadership.*

COACH JOE'S JOURNAL

The effectiveness of the preview is that it is a learning and growing session. It continues to enhance actions for more effective and meaningful relationships among sales team members. The preview to new sales is all about planning and assisting customers on how to make correct buying decisions. A preview can also benefit the whole team if a salesperson is being challenged within the distributor's business by other issues. As an example, a salesperson could volunteer to spend time at the service desk; his or her presence would be an expansion of his or her interest in the distributor's business. Uncovering a problem can lead to coaching the distributor's service rep about relationships and offering an understanding of how to work more effectively with customer complaints. All good salespeople know that service is an important key to continuing sales success. When the salesperson works with his or her peers in preview,

---

sharing information, everyone gains from the experience. They develop ways of using shared information with their distributors, which improves their trust in business relationships.

Conscious value-added salespeople look for opportunities to get involved. They work smarter, while learning and contributing. They are value-added extensions of their customer's business. As a result they influence the people in the distributor business and generate loyalty among them along with a preference for their products and services. Finally, the best work salespeople can do, as an integral part of their customer's business, is to know that as they help their distributors make better and smarter buying decisions, they in turn do the same for their own business. Business growth is secured for everyone, more and more into their shared future.

CHAPTER FIVE

Team Collaboration Unifies and Strengthens Every Member

No one of us is as good as all of us.

At the sales meetings, the preview was all about everyone succeeding during the next business week. Everyone knew that by increasing knowledge and helping one another, they were increasing everyone's ability to be better businesspeople.

After each person presented his or her preview, Kyle would ask if he or she believed in the plan. If the person said yes, Kyle would challenge that team member to commit to its achievement during the next week. This was not for the faint of heart. Commitment is a trusting charge for complete results. Faltering here would mean these team members hadn't taken the time to understand the risks of not completing their planned work—for themselves and for the team. As the process kept improving, team members got better, or they would ultimately, and fortunately, leave the team. Remember, "Pros compete with themselves" first. The pros understood the risks and were committed to taking the right actions now, in anticipation of their expected rewards.

Once team members made their commitments, Kyle would ask them to commit to the entire business sales team that they would achieve their plans. This request was always to motivate them and help them imagine what their successful actions would be like. The intent of commitment is to wipe out any fallback situation that would allow excuses to surface for anyone's lack of performance. By this commitment he or she would be accepting the risks of not achieving his or her planned goals thereby decreasing the business income for him or herself and everyone on the team. The reward for the team would be business growth and the sharing of new learning during the next week's review. This obligation was pure and simple peer pressure—not for the faint of heart. If there was hesitation, it was time for more discussion, focus, and coaching. Kyle was careful not to make this an "end of game" scenario; it was all about digging deeper while growing the talents and abilities of each team member. The purpose is always to continue the development of better businesspeople. Once the commitment was accepted, each team member would sign off on his or her preview.

At the close of the meeting Kyle would ask the opening question again, "What are we learning now that we should be doing more of to keep—and continue to grow—our business and our distributors' businesses now and in the future?" This was when the note-taking had its biggest payback for the team. Everyone would take a turn presenting answers. This recap of business highlights always generated more can-do, winning attitudes among the team members. The momentum kept building. There was contagious gratitude for all the contributions. The dynamics of one idea would sometimes build into a synergy for that idea. Everyone knew ideas were the value-added opportunities for business idea exploration. To keep the motivation high, Kyle always asked someone to make a master set of meeting notes. The notes were then sent out right after the meeting so everyone could make the best use of the sales team collaboration.

Kyle thought, *there is still a sharing defensive shield around each team member. There is a fear, a reluctance to really share everything with everyone in a totally open coaching and nurturing manner that supports truly mutual growth of each and every team member. Do we really want our internal team competitors to become better at business and to exceed their personal sales quota? Isn't it better to be the "Salesperson of the Year"? Or is it better to be on the "#1 Business Sales Team of the Year"? Can we imagine having top-performing salespeople on the #1 Business Sales Team of the Year?* Kyle didn't have the answer yet, but he knew he had to keep expanding the spiral if the team was going to become the #1 Business Sales Team.

COACH JOE'S JOURNAL

In my experiences, once a team begins to understand, know, and believe in their vision, they begin to work with a passion that is not generally talked about in business. It's the energy of love. Love and passion are synonymous. Vision and passion are ever-expanding powers that are contagiously vitalizing, kindling, and nurturing the desire for more. I have worked on business teams where members fed off each other's successes and grew better results to the point that they never thought team members were their competition. New ways of generating business always means constantly improving the present business environment for the better for everyone.

Kyle's story reveals that a sales team cannot be successful anymore if they are not involved in their customers' businesses. Years ago, when I was selling telecommunications systems to the trucking industry, I volunteered to train the dispatchers and drivers on how to be more effective in their use of the two-way radios installed in their trucks. It was an extra effort. It was all about confirming ROI for the investment made to increase profits by accomplishing more while saving time and money. It was all about being more effective. I was the instructor for better use of the product, but I soon found that the students were helping me understand better ways to use the product. Those sessions not only yielded greater customer loyalty, but they also opened the doors to new and different business opportunities for other telecommunications products. After training, I was able to consult with my customers about new possibilities for their business growth, based on what I had learned from their workers. Better relationships developed with everyone in those companies. I became a business resource, receiving more business because I developed an insider company view of ways to improve and grow both their business and mine.

Today those same efforts translate to customizing and training people who buy any product or service. In this business relationship, training is a vital key in proving that you have a mutual vision and the follow-through to help customers not only buy wisely but also realize additional benefits that make their people more effective doing their work with less effort and less money, faster, easier, and better.

CHAPTER SIX

Mutual Growth Generates Unlimited Opportunities

The size of the future you actually experience will largely be determined by one factor: the people you choose to connect with. When you invite people who are truly committed to growth into every aspect of your life, your potential for growth becomes truly unlimited.

Dan Sullivan

The business sales team kept adjusting to the effective changes Kyle was making. They were becoming business salespeople and proud of their new perspective about not being just salespeople. They began questioning and exchanging more and more the business processes of their company and their distributors' businesses. As a result of their actions, they began finding themselves in positions of influence and power.

After several discussions with team members about the preview and review portions of the weekly sales meetings, Kyle announced a change in procedure. From now on the preview and review reports were to be emailed to Kyle no later than 5:00 p.m. on Friday. The Monday morning sales meetings would then be able to start on time and end in time for everyone to begin working their plans for the new week without paperwork distribution delays.

Kyle asked the team to write out their previews and send them in each Friday. Kyle explained, "This will allow the preview, your plan for the new week, to settle in. As you think about it over the weekend, you will be fine-tuning improvements that are surfacing to your plan for actions. You will find yourself consciously and subconsciously amending and solidifying your plan for the new week. By the Monday morning meeting, you will believe and reinforce your plans of action and know them better as well. This means your preview of imagined success will incubate and develop into greater focus, expectation, and commitment to what you know you can make happen."

The preview and review reports were important steps in assuring that each salesperson's performance would continuously improve. Coaching is usually the job of the manager: to influence, nurture and improve performance. However, the changes in the reporting process were yielding information exchanges that got everyone involved, and coaching became everyone's job. This greater collaboration among the team members generated an enthusiasm for the value of their preparation for the new week.

At the close of one of the early Monday morning meetings, Kyle asked if anyone was familiar with the term *Master Mind*. Several hands went up, and some heads nodded in acknowledgement. Years ago, Andrew Carnegie, the great steel magnate, asked Napoleon Hill to study the successful habits of great businesspeople. Hill soon discovered that chief among Carnegie's habits was what he called his Master Mind law of success. Briefly stated, Master Mind is *"a mind that is developed through the harmonious cooperation of two or more people who ally themselves for the purpose of accomplishing any given task."* Consider the board of directors of any company, for example; they do their best work in a spirit of sharing their expertise and in cooperation for the purpose of accomplishing any given task before the board.

In a similar manner, the business sales team was now being commissioned to use its *Master Mind* to become a business sales team. Kyle wanted the team to understand that their collective team spirit, freely sharing and exchanging their knowledge and expertise, would continue to enable and empower every team member to become a better business salesperson.

As Kyle finished, there were a lot of eager faces; people liked what they were hearing. But Kyle could also read the faces of a few who were clearly afraid of this uncertain outcome and how it would impact them. Some needed to know more; there was not unanimous buy-in to what he was proposing. Kyle knew he had some explaining to do. What is the impact on me individually? And, how can I benefit? Otherwise, I'm not sure that I want to be on this team! The change Kyle was proposing was threatening, and some were convinced they needed to protect themselves. They didn't buy in before, and now they did not want to be on this team!

Figure 5. Effectiveness, doing the right thing now, along with "Master Mind," open and sharing interactions, is developed with Mutual Trust because the desire for business success is the interdependent contagious power of the whole team.

COACH JOE'S JOURNAL

Individual competitive drives usually win over collaboration on weak teams that lack a vision of mutual success. Remember, "Pros compete with themselves." To overcome fear of individual losses, team members need to know that ultimately they will benefit from the sharing of their closely held information. On the most successful team I served, everyone was symbiotic but coachable first and foremost. The reward is being coachable by team members who understand that the vision means ultimate success for every member and the whole team. *One for all and all for one* is the ultimate team success pros want—or they won't participate. The team vision, then, is a contagious governing power for success. Members who remain centered on their individual performances are never winners of a winning team. Internally, team members who work

---

with professional competitive drives while being collaborative with other team members learn that mutual winning actions lead them to new levels of their own professionalism. This understanding of "right and now" effective contributions nurtures the leadership strengths of the pros to levels they were not aware they possessed. None of this happens without *trust*. Buy-in to the proven "Master Mind" theory yields the mutual trust, which expands the mutual exchange of information vital to growth and business success of the team. The symbiotic exchanges are always spirited as the vision for the anticipated rewards and consequences for the risks to be taken are challenged and then understood. Once they are agreed upon as the right and effective actions, the entire team progressively unites and supports each other for the ultimate success of our vision.

CHAPTER SEVEN

Ownership Is Accountability *Now!*

People can only be held accountable once they have been given the means and the ability to contribute. If they have the means and ability, they should be appropriately punished or rewarded for their performance.

Etsko Schuitema

Kyle announced, "As a salesperson, you have always been responsible for making your assigned quota. When you performed at quota, you were rewarded with a bonus. Your efforts over the quota period yielded your performance bonus. To place greater emphasis on what we do for ourselves and our company, I am now changing the name of the bonus program. It will now be called the Sales Business Risks and Rewards program. Each team member's business sales bonus will be announced as if given at the beginning of each quarter. It will be payable at 100 percent, or possibly lower, at the end of the quarter, based on each member's contribution or noncontribution over the quarter. It is yours to lose—not to win!"

There was an immediate uproar. Many questions were being asked. What did Kyle mean "yours to lose"?

Kyle explained, "Everyone has one hundred shares at risk, to be maintained or, in the event of a previous loss, regained. At the end of each weekly meeting, everyone will vote on the performance of each team member's contribution or lack of contribution using a specifically designed scorecard to determine shares lost or gained. At the close of the quarter, the remaining percentage of each member's originally invested one hundred shares will be distributed. Votes of shares will be made known at our third weekly meeting and at every meeting after that. Everyone will know whether his or her vote share is on course for the maximum—or less—bonus money. It will also be a time for each team member to know how much the team values his or her contributions. Are you an active or passive mutually contributing member of the team? By the team vote, if you lose a percentage of your shares, it will be your opportunity to increase your business contributions and share more so you can improve your percentage or get back to 100 percent. This business bonus is all about each member's accountability for the risks and rewards being acted on. It is the effect of sharing our team knowledge and efforts—to help us all accomplish more business for our company and for our distributors. Let me repeat, as the voting progresses, each team member will know and have the opportunity to keep his or her reward shares or lose them through the ongoing weekly votes by all the team members. In the final analysis, this is a better way to keep improving our mutual business, and we all benefit by moving closer to becoming the number-one business sales team in the country."

Kyle knew from a sales training manager experience he had attended that sales teams on average consist of four types of players: the star, the rising star, the average, and the laggard. Most sales teams and business teams today dangle a bonus plan that can be achieved at the end of a defined period. As a result, the star and rising star players usually have leading edges, such as being goal driven and having strong work ethics and personal motivation for success. As pros, they compete with themselves. The result is that they work hard and smart to achieve their rewards.

Average players know that if they apply themselves they can earn the maximum bonus or a good portion of it. An average player's incentive is no less important than those of the star and rising star players; it's just that average players depend on circumstances for their reward, rather than making the circumstances right for their success. The result is that these players can be above average from time to time but cannot always be depended on to maximize their rewards for their efforts.

Finally we come to the less-than-average player, the laggard, who just puts in enough effort to be productive while playing on excuses of all kinds about why circumstances are not quite right for his or her success. This player has a job and might serve well when and if he or she finds the right calling. This type of player often consumes a major portion of an ineffective manager's time. Unfortunately, ineffective managers often give these players too much time, which sends the wrong message to the performing players. The effective manager spends time with the average players, coaching and supporting their right efforts, while nurturing the stars and rising stars to continue to be at their best. They also serve as smart working models to the average players who want to move up.

Once a leader/manager understands star players, rising star players, and average players, they spend most of their time with the average players. Successful teams are consistently moving average players to rising star and star status, while helping laggards find other opportunities as quickly as they are identified.

This "ownership rewards for risks taken" process plays out with the known truth that average people will do everything possible to keep from losing—but will not always work harder for the possible gain of rewards. The fear of failure or loss of earnings is greater than the desire for promised gains if the right circumstances happen. It's not about what circumstances happened; it's all about *making* circumstances happen!

> *Circumstances don't make the man. Rather, they reveal the man to himself.*
>
> —James Allen

After the program was implemented, the weekly meetings increased with intensity and commitment. Knowing what one could lose had a greater impact on the level of everyone's business and sales performance. People didn't want to lose what they knew was their share of the business reward already. Now there was greater clarity of planned risks taken and the rewards gained from the right actions. Because they knew what they could keep, they were proactive with actions that eliminated any loss. As team members adapted and got better at risk management, maintaining their reward or earning back losses for their efforts had both personal and team value. No one wanted to lose what they clearly knew they could have at the end of the quarter.

Kyle's recurring vision question was a solid mantra for the entire team: "What are we learning now that we should be doing more of to keep—and continue to grow—our business and our distributors' businesses now and in the future?" The results began to show at the distributor level. The salespeople were now working and being invited to work with more departments and people in the distributors' businesses. This gave them access to the business that truly raised their professional status to business consultants. They were no longer order takers. They were value-added businesspeople working in smarter ways to generate new opportunities for business successes.

At the same time, back in their own company, their internal relationships were skyrocketing. They were earning the right to be more prosperous. The sales team kept increasing the amount of business and competitive knowledge. These business successes assisted them with increases in their business while overcoming threats from the competition. Better strategies followed with better actions that added greater value and quality to the product offerings. Their value-added efforts allowed for price to be maintained. The sales team was now being viewed more closely as a working partner in each and every one of their distributors' businesses.

Relationships escalated and became more interdependent among the sales team members. This was also happening within the distributors' businesses. Collaboration was contagious. All team members became more open about what they were doing together. There was more and better cooperation, sharing, seeking advice—no one wanted to miss out when discussions centered on some idea or business development or when improvement was being generated.

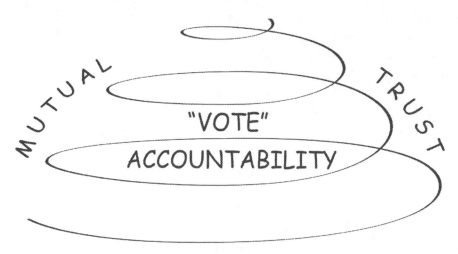

Figure 6. Accountability and Voting with Mutual Trust

By their vote, the team rewards contributors with continued earned employment, and gives notice of rewards to the contributors, while sending an alert to noncontributors that they have not only lost money but are also placing at risk their continuing employment on the team.

COACH JOE'S JOURNAL

In our current economic storm, entrepreneurs and business leaders are particularly concerned about financial resources and how to use them wisely. Scorecard systems are customized and being used more and more today. When incentive bonuses are freely given—or automatically expected—they blow budgets and erode the bottom line inordinately. These same easy bonuses can cause great trust erosion when earnings seem to be automatic dispersions, given for just being on the job, whether you are a star or a laggard. The negative term called upon most often is 'playing politics.' That's why earnings that are calculated against risks taken and winning actions pursued readily receive acceptance by all members of the company team. We are all more sensitive to loss today. More and more smart companies today are openly sharing their financial concerns to sustain the company and their employees. Companies are exercising greater financial caution because of the economic uncertainties in business today.

In the worst financial cases, companies have overextended their businesses and cannot leverage their good work for the necessary money they need from investors or banking institutions. When this happens they are forced to take drastic actions to shore up losses. In the short term, this usually means cutting the most expensive costs first as that has the greatest impact on the bottom line. Unfortunately, that always means cutting people, thereby eliminating their salaries and benefits. This is always a painful decision for everyone; and business hindsight usually indicates a lack of openness and sharing of financial information that would have yielded greater involvement and commitment from all the people in the business. When you know ahead of time that your job could be on the line, you are tuned in to work harder and smarter

---

to generate the gains that will keep your company on a successful path and keep you gainfully employed. When entrepreneurial leaders share this information, it yields a sense of accountability to each other and ownership by the whole company team, as they understand the risks they must take to earn the rewards of a successful team. Most importantly, companies today do not want to have to lose the developed value-added talent of their hard- and smart-working employees. They are openly admitting it. In the knowledge era we live in, people are smarter and more able than ever before. People are being recognized, valued more, and treasured more than any other business resource. If you understand this, it's no longer machines that make the difference in a business. It's the mentally enabled and empowered people. They are the enabling and empowering economic momentum of today's business successes.

PERFORMING—
EXTRORDINARY TIMES
DURING TEAM UNITY

CHAPTER EIGHT

Emerging Team Member Leadership

Opportunity dances with those who are already on the dance floor.

H. Jackson Brown Jr.

As mutual trust increased, team members started taking leadership roles on various issues that they were sincerely interested in. Better performances resulted from team member buy-in and actions. Passion made them champions and leaders of business issues to the rest of the team; and mutual trust in team member commitment, agreement, and support led to greater team accountability .

Leadership is the ability to get other people to do the things you want them to do because they want to do them.

When marketing ideas were discussed, for instance, a salesperson who was *passionate* about marketing became the go-to person for developing, sharing, influencing, nurturing, and exchanging the sales team's work with the marketing department. When one of the distributors began having problems with the co-op advertising program and the delayed reimbursement for their local advertisements, the sales team representative took charge of the issue and worked directly with the marketing department. After discussion and review, a better process emerged in which the distributor was able to receive the co-op dollars more quickly while being able to honor rebates in the store at the time of purchase.

The law of reciprocity kicked in because the more this was done for others, the more the sales team received and was recognized by their own marketing department and the distributors' marketing departments. As a result of his or her efforts, the sales team representative was able to work with the distributor to pilot an upgrade, an exchange program that benefited both marketing departments. These efforts were recognized more and more, and the sales business team began realizing rewards for their shared insight exchanges. Internally, their own company began recognizing them as the only emerging business sales team in the country.

Timely scheduling and delivery of products was a very critical area where sales needed to beat the competition. The preview work done by the sales team met with complimentary acclaim and became a generating factor with the manufacturing, scheduling, and shipping departments. Product could now profitably be moved from "work in progress" status to "available inventory" status, it allowed for more products to be built on time and within the scheduled shipping date with less risk to the cost of inventory. Manufacturing very quietly created a no-risk "set aside" inventory, predicated on the accuracy and consistency of sales forecasted and sales completed by the business sales team.

Einstein said, "What you think about expands," and so it was for the business sales team. They were developing greater knowledge and understanding of the risks and rewards of the company and distributors' businesses. They were operating 'in the zone' with the highest levels of trust. Very confidently they were developing and growing continuous value-added improvements because of their mutual trust. Their intentions became a synergy of encouraging and nurturing actions. One person's success was everyone's success.

COACH JOE'S JOURNAL

In many cases, field sales teams rarely get an opportunity to know and understand all the departments that contribute to their companies' final products. A cell phone, for example, just appears to be a simple product. You buy the parts and then assemble them. However, in reality, some parts can be bought but others have to be engineered, designed, manufactured, and have software applications embedded in them so they can be part of the assembly. Another phase of production is quality control, packaging, inventory control, scheduling, shipping, and receiving. When you think about all the functions of a company that sells products, you start to realize that it is a giant puzzle that operates with teams of people who, working together, become the company team. A successful business client of mine summed it up this way: "You know the philosophy of our company comes from you teaching us about puzzle building which we have adopted as our description of what our company is all about. THANK YOU!"

CHAPTER NINE

Effectiveness: Achieving Mutual Growth

You won't get all my business until you understand that I am an extension of your business.

—Sam Walton

Kyle noticed during preview discussions that a new competitive edge had started to emerge. It was apparent, but no one could quite grasp what the next best actions were to take with the distributors. The distributors' salespeople were, in reality, retail service technicians. They knew enough about the products to answer questions but did not know how to help if the customer was price shopping. Dropping the retail price was not an option; consequently, there was a minimum of sales skill available—let alone being used with any awareness.

Rather than consulting with the customer about buying value or quality, it was simply left to the customer to buy or not to buy. This opened the door for the customer to buy any competitive offering or, worse yet, walk out and buy from the distributor's competitor. In the worst-case scenario, no sale was made, and everyone lost the business. The distributors' salespeople relied heavily on the manufacturer's marketing, brand-name recognition, or point-of-sale posters to assist customers in making buying decisions. Assisting each customer in making a choice was foreign and uncomfortable to them. They expected and relied on the customers to educate themselves about the products they wanted to buy.

As a consequence, three out five people became customers, but two out of five people simply walked out, not making any purchase. That translated to 40 percent of the business potential being lost. The distributors' salespeople did not know how to help customers save time investigating their purchases properly. As a result, in some cases there was no sale for any business member in the sales chain. Customers needed the right assistance in choosing the benefits that would help them make the right buying decision on the spot.

Understanding this business opportunity meant knowing that the sale was a mutual win for both the distributors and Kyle's sales team. More product sales by the distributors would mean an increase of 40 percent in sales for the distributors and an increase in market share for the business sales team. The more they could assist distributors in this effort, the more sales could be closed for all the business teams. The market was booming, and this was a great opportunity for new sales advancement. How could Kyle's team make every sales interaction a mutually positive success? What could they do to get the distributors tuned into the mutual opportunity for themselves and their customers?

Armed with this information, Kyle began working with the sales team. In no time at all, they developed a basic sales consulting training course; it was centered on selling their company products through the distributors' salespeople, who consulted with customers to help them make their best purchase 'Right Now!' The training session was simply called Buyer Consultant 101.

Kyle was the sales manager and sales coach for his sales team. Everyone looked to Kyle, so it was natural for him to take the lead in training the sales team on how to present and coach Buyer Consultant 101 training to the distributors' people (who would now be referred to as buyer consultants). It wasn't easy—even with the possibility of a 40 percent increase in sales. So, while everyone knew this was a key element in their quest to achieve greater sales success that could set them apart from their competition, some salespeople were reluctant to make an attempt at training their distributors' salespeople. Kyle's vision now included a new leadership role for the sales team that would put them way out in front of the competition. This value-added business service could slow down new competitors entering the market and set current competitors on their heels for a long time to come.

The value-added business services would benefit everyone. This was maximum mutual benefit for the customer, the distributor, and their own company.

Kyle's vision for the team raised the bar to a new level. Everyone understood the vision and was behind him in the effort. The problem was they were *behind* him! So to accommodate the sales team's reluctance to train, Kyle had to do the right thing now. He became the trainer in reserve to his role as the sales manager and coach. To his delight, the distributors went for the idea and wanted him doing the training sessions. After all, they knew Kyle was the sales manager and coach of the sales team. After a short period of time, Kyle's sales team was outselling sales teams in other parts of the country. Headquarters was noticing, and they wanted to know more!

COACH JOE'S JOURNAL

Early in my career I had the good fortune of transitioning from selling directly to customers. I was selling a product that was confusing to first-time users, and the customers needed help buying. Just like with cell phones today, the product has more functions than most people know how to use. To be effective, I had to consult with customers and help them get the best return on their investments. I began doing extra work, training the customers' workers in how to use our products effectively. Their work was made easier, making them more productive and profitable. This translated into great ROI, Return On Investment justification, which led to more referrals and new sales.

When selling through distributors, this carries over into a two-step distribution process. The distributors we were working with were available to walk-in prospects but didn't know how to consult with them or—even better—make them feel good about making a purchasing decision. *Buying is usually done emotionally and then justified afterward with the facts.* Consulting, on the other hand, helps the prospect justify with facts and minimizes the emotional questions asked afterward about whether the decision was made too hastily. It reduces the likelihood of buyer's remorse. Helping someone to be a smart buyer breeds confidence in his or her decision

---

and they are more apt to refer others to do business with you. When people buy, they are living testimonials.

Now you can understand why Sam Walton was right: a manufacturer who understands that the distributor of their product is an extension of the manufacturer's business—and who works to ensure more and more sales—generates mutual wins for everyone. And that includes the final customer, who is not sold—but buys.

CHAPTER TEN

Speeding Synchronously

Mutual momentum leads to exponential opportunities.

The more Kyle trained the distributors' salespeople, the more knowledge and information was shared that was of mutual benefit. Buyer Consultant 101 was a big hit and quickly added to Kyle's workload. He absolutely loved every minute of the training opportunity. Training others provided him with growth factors that were sometime elusive in the average business relationship. There were more benefits to working at the grassroots level of the distributors' businesses; the salespeople asked questions, shared ideas, and helped generate new insights about how to make more product sales.

In addition to Kyle, the local business sales team member was always present and active during Kyle's training sessions. He or she reinforced the training by acting as co-trainers. This also made him or her a coach with the distributor's salespeople after Kyle left. Kyle was training and assisting his team's learning as well as that of the distributor's salespeople. Increasingly, the sales team wanted to know more about what Kyle was learning. This information added to the opening questions at Kyle's weekly business sales team meetings: What are we learning now that we should be doing more of to keep—and continue to grow—our business and our distributors' businesses now and in the future?

Success is not for the timid. It is for those who seek guidance, make decisions, and take decisive action.

Jose Silva

Kyle shared information with the business sales team, and the team shared and spread the good news with marketing, manufacturing, and other allies within the company. Sharing enabled all members of the company team to generate business strategies and actions that improved sales projections and sales performance. Value-added services were stacking up everywhere. All facets of the distributors' businesses were learning and growing too. On a competitive note, Kyle's sales team was increasing market penetration and the company's share of the market. The 40 percent projection for increasing sales was being confirmed by their new efforts with the distributors. Adding to this was the fact that not only were they beating the competition, they were outselling their peer sales teams in the rest of the country.

As a team reaches its highest level, they are in sync with each other. Love, passion for the work being done, is like an energy drink. When people are working with passion, increasingly they find themselves doing more for and with less … faster, easier, better.

The business continued to grow and prosper more than ever before. Everyone appreciated Kyle, but strangely Kyle himself felt less needed. Truly, everyone on the team now had the opportunity to lead. Kyle was becoming a part-time manager and coach. The team had many leadership roles now. He was still the named leader of the team, but more importantly, he was now also recognized as a contributing leader-member of the business sales team.

When other sales managers in the country questioned Kyle about the secret to his sales team successes, Kyle willingly shared copies of the Buyer Consultant 101 training program. He encouraged the other sales teams to capitalize on training their distributors. He was quick to explain that it was a dynamic value-added service that offered everyone mutual benefits, as the competition was not yet able to provide training to the distributors.

Headquarters promoted Buyer Consultant 101 training, and it became known as the best new idea for sales growth in the country. Buyer Consultant 101 was the leading edge, offering mutual benefits that increased everyone's bottom line. That included the distributors' new customers who received their ROI the same day instead of waiting, shopping around, or never buying.

On the surface, sales training looked easy, but the wrinkle was that very few company salespeople anywhere in the country were comfortable transitioning to the role of sales trainer for their distributors. Kyle knew this from the experiences on his own sales team. The salespeople all knew and understood how to sell, but they were uncomfortable standing up and transferring their knowledge as subject-matter experts to their distributors' salespeople. Kyle did not want to be a crutch for his sales team, but he wanted to make sure they had every advantage to achieve the vision of becoming the number-one business sales team in the country. Kyle was now the sales manager, coach, and leader for sales training for his business sales team.

As the word continued to filter out to all the other sales teams, Kyle was invited to their sales meetings to do a Buyer Consultant 101 "train the trainer" workshop. This was always done with the unselfish hope that there would be a contagious effort by every salesperson to train their distributors' salespeople. Appreciation and acceptance of the program as a new way to generate more business was good, but in the end the effort was not as successful as Kyle had hoped for, for the same reasons that Kyle had experienced with his own sales team: business continued to be good, so the salespeople remained confident that they were getting all the business they could. It defied Kyle's understanding and raised the question of why salespeople wouldn't push harder for more sales.

When he pressed the issue, the answer he received was the following: "We are the biggest and the best. Exceeding sales quota is good, but manufacturing has to ship more products faster." Added to this was the normal fear of public speaking. And the issue was made more complex by the fear about training one distributor in a particular town rather than another. When it was done, the other distributor almost always asked, "Why weren't we first?" Salespeople agonized over the concern that any preferential treatment in offering Buyer Consultant 101 might alienate other distributors and open the door to the competition.

This anticipated outcome usually ended in a request for Kyle to come out and train the other distributors. After conducting several training sessions for other teams, Kyle knew that doing training for the other teams in the rest of the country was not the outcome he had intended. It took him away from his work with his own sales team. So he declined requests and retreated back to his own sales team where he was happy doing what he loved: managing, coaching, and training his sales team with the goal of becoming the number-one business sales team in the country. Actions speak louder than words. The team actions were better and better, mounting to the biggest payoff. Every team member's performance was at a record high.

> *Most people come to work well prepared, well motivated, and wanting to reach their potential. A primary issue today is helping managers understand that it's not their job to supervise or to motivate but to liberate and enable. You have to look at leadership through the eyes of the followers. Lech Walesa told Congress that there is a declining world market for words. He's right. The only thing the world believes is behavior, because we all see it instantaneously. None of us may preach anymore. We must behave.* (Max De Pree, retired CEO, Herman Miller, Inc.)

Figure 7. Breaking Through

Individuals on a team are usually independent competitive performers—too busy taking care of "me" to make the breakthrough necessary to become a great team. Contrary to that, great teams know their success is a vision in common unity, intentionally imagining, with focus and commitment to their eventual breakthrough. It moves up with their mutual engagement, continuously renewing and improving the whole team in a spirit of mutual trust. This "spiraling up" is a shattering process that develops and elevates every member, resulting in the Great Team.

METAMORPHOSIS—
TRANSCENDING THE EMBRYO OF "ME"

CHAPTER ELEVEN

Benefits of the New "WE"

Find and build on strengths, then organize to make weaknesses irrelevant.
Peter Drucker, *The Effective Executive*

Salespeople can be competitive to a fault. However, when a team works together cooperatively and with accountability, in their environment of mutual trust, they know and understand that the rewards for the risks taken build to a momentum, bringing more victories their way. All their senses tell them and they know the benefits of being a team working in collaboration is a universal truth. At its breakthrough, impossibility is nonexistent. The team's collective thoughts power up and center on their desires, expectations, and, most importantly, imagined outcomes. This confidence of knowing breaks through all barriers; vision is the vortex that pushes for new achievements. This is *positive herd mentality*. Let me be so bold as to paraphrase the words of James Allen, "As *we* think, so shall *we* become." Now as *we* expands with a positive collective spirit operating in mutual trust, the team knows itself better and better. They are all making contributions for the benefit of each other and becoming better and better. *As the team grows to know itself, the members break through—transcending "me"—and together "we" go to breakthrough levels, accomplishing:*

- More in collective abundance
- For less time and money

- Faster, with mutual trust in collaboration
- Easier, with all inclusive talents
- Better, always getting better and better

MORE

The *more* people work as a team, the *more* they achieve. The team working in cooperation, sharing an abundance of talent, accomplishes more than one isolated person working alone. Vision is the rising vortex of focused intention for right actions now. The team communicates more often, more openly, and more freely for their mutual benefit in their common unity. The strength of their diversity is their inclusion. Sharing their talents, time, and money, they do the right thing now with effectiveness and accountability in the spirit of mutual trust. *Welcome to the shared and valued compounding knowledge era.*

FOR LESS

The more people work as a team, the more they get for less. Right timing, right money, and right talent keep adding up to "All Right." The team working together mutually focuses their efforts on doing the right thing now and then doing the thing right the first time. "For less" means investments in time, money, and talent always yields the best returns on investment. This is done with the whole team, in mutually trusting collaboration, previewing and agreeing with right commitments. *Welcome to the shared and valued compounding knowledge era.*

FASTER

The more people work as a team, the more they achieve for less—faster. Cooperation with total inclusion of the diversity of talents generates faster returns more than one person working alone. The vision is the rising contagion of their collective knowledge power. The more they communicate, the faster they understand what needs to be done now. The more the team includes all the available talents, the faster things get done. Team members know and collaborate more in this environment, so the work gets done faster. Team members interdependently and competitively push their pace and their effectiveness with their imagination for the success of the whole team. Imagined successes powers up the excitement and accelerates faster. *Welcome to the shared and valued compounding knowledge era.*

EASIER

The more people work as a team, the more they achieve for less—faster and easier. It becomes easier because the team is unified by a focused, shared, and imagined vision. It's easier because they are internally collaborative and externally competitive. Teamwork is easier because all the members' senses are keyed on supporting, assisting, and mutually coaching each other for greater successes they have imagined collectively. It's easier because of the collaboration of previewing and reviewing all team member goals for the team's mutual benefit. It's also easier because they communicate about and share in all the work resources. The team commits and focuses on talent, time, and money. Teamwork is easier because members nurture each other's expertise and contributions for benefit of the whole team. It is easier because they do the right thing now and they do things right the first time. *Welcome to the shared and valued compounding knowledge era.*

BETTER

The more people work as a team, the more they get done for less—faster, easier, and better. Better is a never-ending game. Better breeds the highest quality and value now, at this moment. Better is the team's collective mind keyed with mutual trust for collaboration and mutual benefit. Better is the mutually collective focus on and commitment to higher imagined results. The results become better and better as the team members synchronize and energize each other to do better. "Better and better" is the moment-to-moment focusing on perpetual and continuous improvements, generating exponential momentum to turn today's impossibilities into tomorrow's possibilities. *Welcome to the shared and valued compounding knowledge era.*

COACH JOE'S JOURNAL

I was mentoring an aspiring leader recently, and she asked about her next step in her leadership journey. We started with a review of knowing herself.

Leadership is a humbling charge. You are the giver. You are passionate, and you love what you do. You trust and are trusted. You are the psychic with a vision. You motivate by your visible and invisible presence. You are the "spirit" of the people. They think they are you, and they don't want to let themselves down. You are their nourishment. You nurture them to be better and better. You offer celebration and purpose by your presence in their lives. Secretly, they sense and imagine their continuous improvements. You are their good fortune, but they are doing it themselves.

True Leaders
Are hardly known by their followers.
Next after them are the leaders
The people know and admire.
After them, those they fear.
After them, those they despise.
To give no trust is to get no trust.
When the work's done right,
With no fuss or boasting,
Ordinary people say,
"Oh, we did it ourselves."

—Lao-Tzu, Chinese poet and philosopher, sixth century BC

CHAPTER TWELVE

Afterword

"WE" did it!

The main ingredient of stardom is the rest of the team.
Coach John Wooden

Time passed. New business strategies and tactics helped the team members become more and more successful. The business sales team was out front, leading the nation in business and sales.

When the national sales meeting took place, the team received recognition as the "Business Sales Team of the Year." The entire team was up on stage to receive the award and have their picture taken as part of the celebration. Later, Kyle had the award and the team picture placed prominently at the entrance to the office, proudly displaying the names of all the contributing team members as the country's number-one business sales team.

And so the story ends. From first-day jitters and team suspicion to previews and reviews, the team worked together by sharing knowledge and creating synergy. The whole team came to know that they were all interdependent team leaders in common unity. Kyle was one leader—just as they all were leaders.

Kyle knew it was easy for a manager and team leader to get caught up in the team success and forget that success is the culmination of *passion* for the plans and activities to which every team member contributed his or her leadership skills. When the ultimate success happens, it's important to understand that the process has many challenges that are addressed along the way by the co-missioning of every team member, with their complimentary inclusion with the whole team, in a Spirit of great common unity. Kyle and the team reflected on their journey to success. Their recall was followed by a jubilant celebration for what they had achieved together.

MEGA-METAMORPHOSIS—
"WE" EQUALS MANY AND NEW BREAKTHROUGHS

CHAPTER THIRTEEN

We Are All Leaders

I want to lead with you leading too!

As time progressed, wherever the former team members found themselves, their common bond was the success they had achieved together developing and growing the first number-one business sales team. That success was a constant reminder of what they knew about their metamorphosis from me to we. *Forming* with the right team members, *Storming* with commitment and agreement for the right actions now, *Performing* with mutual trust, and *Metamorphosis*, they came to know they were all leaders succeeding together.

> *To give anything less than all you've got is to waste the gift*
> Steve Prefontane

Mega-Metamorphosis happens with great teams whenever a work challenge, project, or new business opportunity reaches out for them to join in a vision for imagined success. It happens as quickly as it did in the movie *The Sting*. In the movie, team members were invited by an innate knowing that they were needed with their key complimentary talents for a new mission. Similarly, with team members who have successful experiences, the Mega-Metamorphosis happens with an invite, like a breakthrough from their cocoon of the present moment to an imagined spectacular moment in their future. You can be called; it can all occur—pure and simple—with a mere "twitch of the nose or an affirmative nod." ***SPIRAL UP!***

BONUS MATERIAL #1

I went on a search to become a leader.

I searched high and low. I spoke with authority. People listened. But alas, there was one who was wiser than I, and they followed that individual.

I sought to inspire confidence, but the crowd responded, "Why should I trust you?"

I postured, and I assumed the look of leadership with a countenance that flowed with confidence and pride. But many passed me by and never noticed my air of elegance.

I ran ahead of the others, pointed the way to new heights. I demonstrated that I knew the route to greatness. And then I looked back, and I was alone.

"What shall I do?" I queried. "I've tried hard and used all that I know." And I sat down and pondered long.

And then I listened to the voices around me. And I heard what the group was trying to accomplish. I rolled up my sleeves and joined in the work.

As we worked, I asked, "Are we all together in what we want to do and how to get the job done?"

And we thought together, and we fought together, and we struggled together towards our goal.

I found myself encouraging the fainthearted. I sought the ideas of those too shy to speak out. I taught those who had little skill. I praised those who worked hard. When our task was completed, one of the group turned to me and said, "This would not have been done but for your leadership."

At first I said, "I didn't lead. I just worked with the rest." And then I understood, leadership is not a goal. It's a way of reaching a goal.

I lead best when I help others to go where we've decided to go. I lead best when I help others to use themselves creatively. I lead best when I forget about myself as leader and focus on my group ... their words and their goals.

To lead is to serve ... to give ... to achieve together.

Anonymous

BONUS MATERIAL #2

You Are a Marvel

When will we teach our children in school
What they are?
We should say to each of them:
Do you know what you are?
You are a Marvel.
You are unique.
In all the world there is no other child exactly like you.
In the millions of years that have passed
There has never been another child like you.
And look at your body –
What a wonder it is!
Your legs, your arms, your cunning fingers,
The way you move!
You may become
a Shakespeare, a Michelangelo, a Beethoven.
You have the capacity for anything.
Yes, You are a marvel.

Pablo Casals

BONUS MATERIAL #3

TO MY FELLOW SWIMMERS:
Here is a river flowing now very fast.
It is so great and swift that there are those
who will be afraid,
who will try to hold on to the shore and will suffer greatly.
Know that the river has its destination.
The elders say we must let go of the shore.
Push off into the middle of the river,
and keep our heads above water.
And I say see who is there with you and celebrate.
At this time in history,
we are to take nothing personally,
least of all ourselves, for the moment we do,
our spiritual growth and journey come to a halt.
The time of the lone wolf is over.
Gather yourselves.
Banish the word struggle from your attitude and vocabulary.
All that we do now must be done
in a sacred manner and in celebration.
For we are the ones we have been waiting for.

From the Elders of the Hopi Nation
Oraibi, Arizona, June 8, 2000

BONUS MATERIAL #4

Here's a free, Self Coaching example for more effective sales calls

PAR 3

Coaching for Successes on Every Sales Call

- Preview
- Act out the Call
- R
  - Review
  - Reflect
  - Re-Act

Go to our website for a free, detailed download: team2learn.com

ABOUT THE AUTHOR

Joseph P. "Coach Joe" Sasso is the president of Team 2 LEarn, Inc. Joe's career has included work in sales and marketing, management, and leadership of a global business consulting, training, and development team. The team developed thirty-seven training programs for business, and ultimately, the people who received training numbered in the hundreds of thousands. One of Joe's most prized awards was being elected to the "Galvin Masters." This prestigious title is awarded by peer  election to less than 2 percent of the Sales Professionals at Motorola Inc.

Today Joe continues to work in his passion through Team 2 LEarn, Inc. (www.team2learn.com). He customizes training and leads business retreats focusing on Sales, Authentic Leadership and Teamwork. He is a business certified Emotional Intelligence Mentor with EQ Mentor. Joe is a certified John C. Maxwell Coach, Trainer, and Speaker.